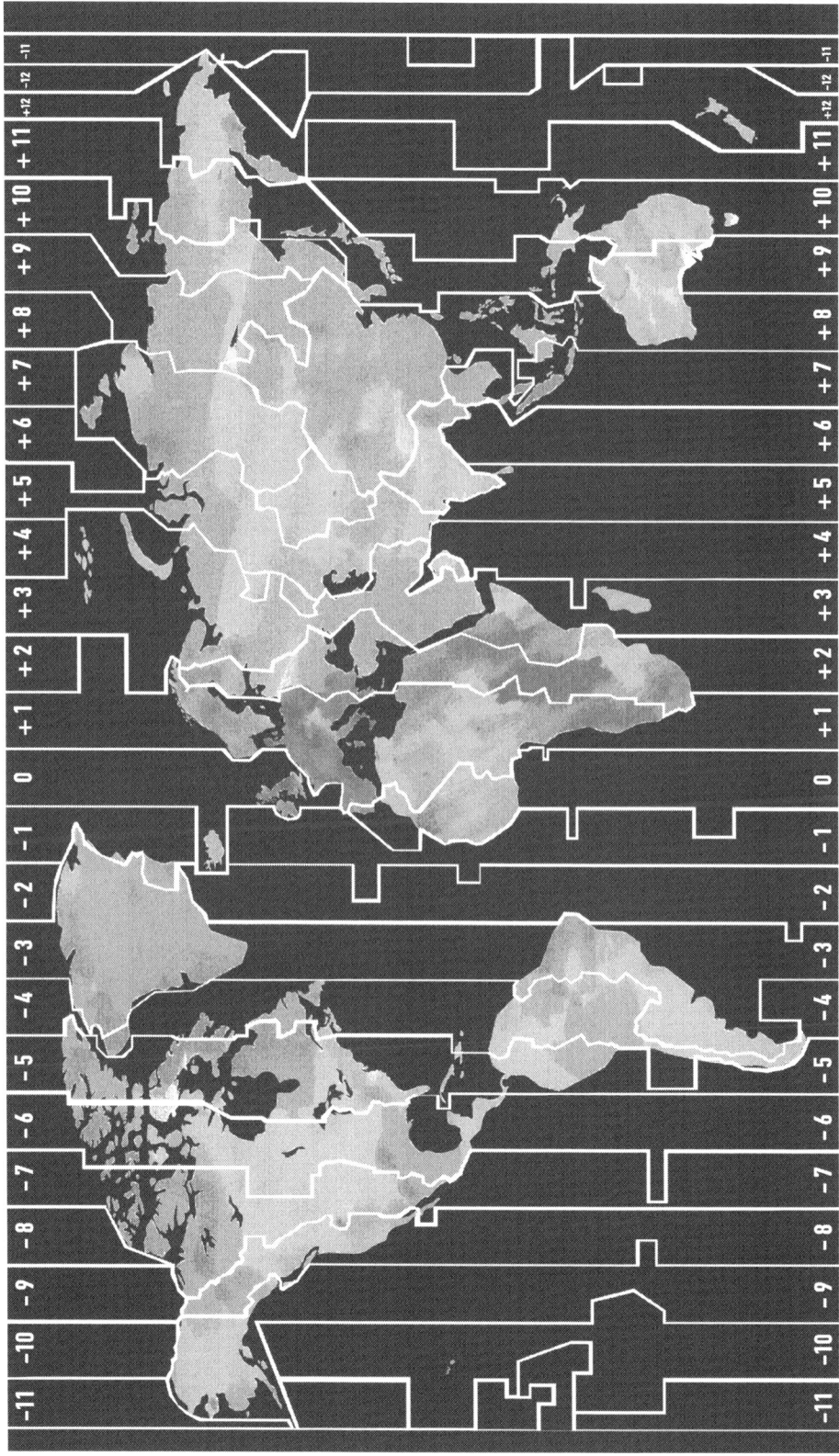

TIME ZONE MAP

DESTINATION(S):

GOOD TO KNOW ABOUT REGION AND CULTURE:

# PACKING LIST

# TO DO BEFORE LEAVING

# BUCKET LIST

# BUDGET

|  |  |
|---|---|
|  |  |

| TOTAL: | TOTAL: |

LOCATION:                                    DATE:

DESTINATION(S):

GOOD TO KNOW ABOUT REGION AND CULTURE:

# PACKING LIST

# TO DO BEFORE LEAVING

# BUCKET LIST

- [ ]
- [ ]
- [ ]
- [ ]
- [ ]
- [ ]
- [ ]
- [ ]
- [ ]
- [ ]
- [ ]
- [ ]
- [ ]
- [ ]
- [ ]
- [ ]
- [ ]
- [ ]
- [ ]
- [ ]
- [ ]
- [ ]
- [ ]
- [ ]
- [ ]
- [ ]
- [ ]
- [ ]
- [ ]
- [ ]
- [ ]

# BUDGET

|  |  |
|---|---|
|  |  |

| TOTAL: | TOTAL: |

LOCATION:                    DATE:

41923824R00070

Printed in Poland
by Amazon Fulfillment
Poland Sp. z o.o., Wrocław